T0197586

WestBow Press books may be ordered through booksellers or by contacting:

WestBow Press
A Division of Thomas Nelson & Zondervan
1663 Liberty Drive
Bloomington, IN 47403
www.westbowpress.com
844-714-3454

ISBN: 978-1-4908-7159-2 (sc)
ISBN: 978-1-4908-7160-8 (e)

Library of Congress Control Number: 2015903533

Print information available on the last page.

WestBow Press rev. date: 01/23/2021

WESTBOW
PRESS®
A DIVISION OF THOMAS NELSON
& ZONDERVAN

Acknowledgements

Brenda G. Rice (Editor)
Tyler Carter (Editor)
Whitney Menogan (Editor)

This book is for Children ages 12 -Up

Once upon a time, there was a little boy named Tommie. Tommie was a very bad boy because he did things kids should never do. At school or whenever he was around smart kids, he would make fun of them. Sometimes he would even take their lunch money. It was all fun to him and it made him feel like he was tough. Tommie hung with older kids he called his "friends." Tommie and the older boys would get into all kinds of trouble. He felt like a tough guy when he did things the older kids did. Tommie never stopped to think that all the things they did were wrong.

When Tommie was in the fifth grade, he started missing days from school. His parents did not know he was not going to school when he left home each morning. School work seemed hard to him, and he felt embarrassed because he thought he was not smart and could not read and write like the other kids. He was afraid they would laugh and tease him. Instead of talking to his parents about his fears and getting help with his classwork, Tommie would simply avoid going to school as often as he could. These were days he would get into mischief with his friends.

One afternoon, Tommie made a decision that changed his life forever. He decided to go along with his friends to break into a home to steal video games and all the money they could find. What Tommie and the boys did not know was that the home had an alarm that made a very loud noise, like a siren, whenever a door or window was opened. Only the people who lived in the house knew how to turn the loud noise of the alarm off. It could be heard by everyone who lived on the street. It also sounded at the police station to let them know someone had entered the home who did not live there. The police hurried to the home to capture the intruders. When Tommie and the boys saw them, they became very frightened. Tommie ran out the back door all the way home.

Once at home, Tommie hid underneath his bed shaking and afraid for hours. He thought, "Man, I should have gone to school!" Finally, Tommie heard the school bus arrive as it dropped kids off in his neighborhood. He thought for certain he had escaped the police. As soon as Tommie heard the kids' voices, he ran outside to join them. To his surprise, the police were also outside. When they saw him, they quickly arrested him, put him in the police car, and took him to jail. While riding, he thought, "If only I had gone to school, I would not be in trouble and headed to jail."

He wondered why his friends would tell on him. He had gotten away, but they had given the police his name and told them where he lived. Tommie thought the boys could be trusted not to tell on him because they were his friends. He learned a lot about friendship that day.

When Tommie's parents received a call from the police, they rushed to the police station. He knew he was in a lot of trouble. Tommie was released to go home, and thereafter, punished by his parents for not going to school and breaking into someone's home. His parents could not understand how he could make such bad choices. Tommie could have gone to jail for a very long time instead of being free to go home. He was also not allowed to hang with the older boys again. Though Tommie knew he never wanted to go to jail again, this life changing experience still did not discourage him from being mischievous.

Upon returning to school, Tommie continued his misconduct. He felt he needed to maintain his tough- guy image. He clowned around, bothered the other kids, and continued taking lunch money. Then one day, Tommie threw paper at the teacher while her back was turned. The teacher was furious with Tommie, and she sent him to the principal's office. By this time, the principal was so frustrated with Tommie's behavior that she expelled him from the school. Afterwards, Tommie went from one school to another and was expelled again and again because of his bad behavior.

It seemed no one wanted Tommie around. Even the parents in the neighborhood did not want their children to interact with him. He was lonely and had no one to play with. This soon made him discover the game of basketball because this was something he could play alone. Tommie practiced every day until he became very good at the sport.

One day while the other kids were in school, Tommie was walking around the neighborhood bouncing his ball and searching for someone to play basketball with. Suddenly, a car pulled up and a man rolled down his window and said, "How are you doing, little man? My name is Coach Tommy Ford. What is your name? " Tommie noticed that he and Coach Ford had something in common— they shared the same first name. Coach Ford asked, "Have you ever played basketball for a team?" Tommie replied, "No." Coach Ford then asked him if he would like to play for his team. Tommie accepted and joined the basketball team. As time passed and Coach Ford watched him play, he realized that Tommie was really good at the sport. For the first time, Tommie began to enjoy himself while playing ball. His parents were very happy to see him involved in doing something good.

Tommie's parents soon found him a new school to attend. He did not like the thought of going back to school. All of his fears returned. He thought of what the kids might say and that they might laugh at him once they learned he could not read well or write. Coach Ford told him he could not play basketball if he did not attend school every day and stay out of trouble. Tommie eagerly agreed to do both. He would have done anything to play basketball.

Although Tommie stayed out of trouble at school, he did not complete any of his classwork. Instead, he would sleep in class and wait for the bell to ring. His only thought was to go to basketball practice with Coach Ford's team. Then one day, Tommie found out his school was holding basketball tryouts. But since his grades were bad, he could not participate. Tommie was told his grades would have to improve in order for him to try out. He could not see how his grades could improve and became frustrated. He began to feel school was not for him.

BASKETBALL TRYOUTS

TODAY!

By this time, Tommie's self-esteem was very low. One morning, he saw his old friends on the corner laughing and joking. He ran to greet them, and they all shook hands. Tommie did not know that he was about to experience another life-changing experience. He was, again, in the wrong place at the wrong time. One of the guys shouted, "You guys want to see something?"

"Yes," they anxiously replied. The boy pulled out a gun. Tommie yelled, "Put that away before someone gets hurt!" As the boy put the gun in his pocket, it fired. "Boom!" Tommie felt a sharp pain and realized he had been shot in the foot. He yelled so loud that a passer-by heard him and rushed him to the hospital.

AHHH!!! MY FOOT!!!

Once at the hospital, Tommie's parents were called. When they arrived, he could see that they were scared and disappointed that he had not gone to school as he should have. The doctor had taken an x-ray and showed it to Tommie and his parents. The sad news they were told was that Tommie may not be able to move his foot again. They all cried after hearing the news. Tommie wailed and yelled, "Why didn't I just go to school? Why didn't I just go to school?"

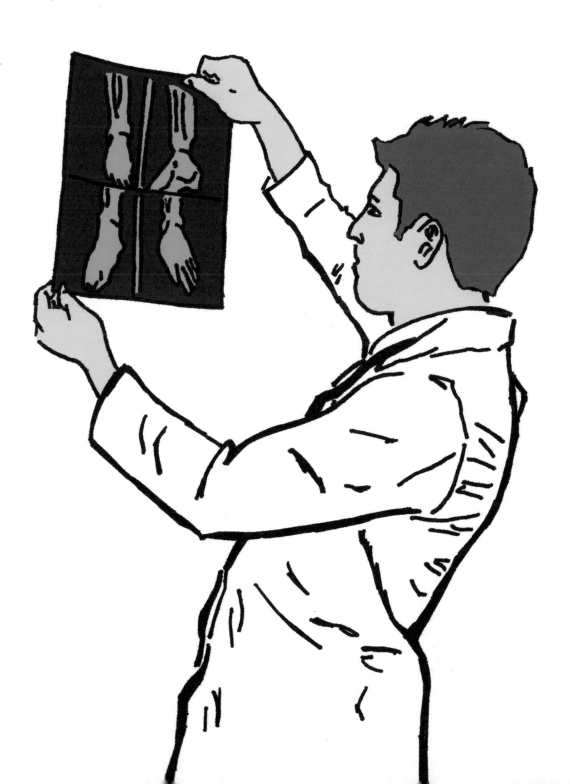

Tommie's parents took him home and laid him in the bed. The doctor told him to get bed rest. He could not go outside nor play basketball. So, Tommie laid in bed and cried and cried. In the middle of the night, Tommie awoke and cried out to God in a letter that read: "Dear God, please help me to get back on my feet to play basketball. I will do well in school, and I will study every day."

As weeks passed, Tommie began to walk; eventually, he began to run. God heard his cry! Tommie now realized that those he considered his friends were not the kind of friends he should have. None of the guys he got into mischief with came to see him while he was home on bed rest.

When Tommie was well enough, he went back to school with a renewed attitude. He would raise his hand and participate in class; stay after school to get extra help; and when school ended for the day, he would go straight home to do his homework. Tommie realized he was not dumb, or illiterate, because his grades were improving. All he needed to do was apply himself—do his very best, believe in himself, and do the right things. As a result of his hard work, he was able to play on the school's basketball team. How overjoyed he was!

That school year, Tommie played ball very well. He was so exceptional on the basketball court that he received a full scholarship to play college basketball. Tommie's future was so bright! His parents did not have to pay anything with him receiving the scholarship. When Tommie began college, he knew he had to do well in his classes by studying and making good grades. So, that's what he did. He put studying first and basketball second. By doing this, he knew he would have a second plan in case his plans and career in basketball came to an end. Tommie knew he could have a great life if he did well in college and graduated.

Once Tommie graduated from college, he returned to his hometown and became a teacher in the same school system that expelled him when he was a child. The teachers who remembered Tommie from his school days were amazed by his progress and the exceptional leader he had become.

Now Tommie is screaming,

"IF I CAN DO IT, YOU CAN DO IT; IF TOMMIE CAN DO IT, WE CAN DO IT!"

Remember Tommie's four B's and the quote he lives by: Be confident, Be determined, Be motivated, and Be yourself!
"I cannot walk in my future, with my foot in my past."

ALERT!
ALERT!

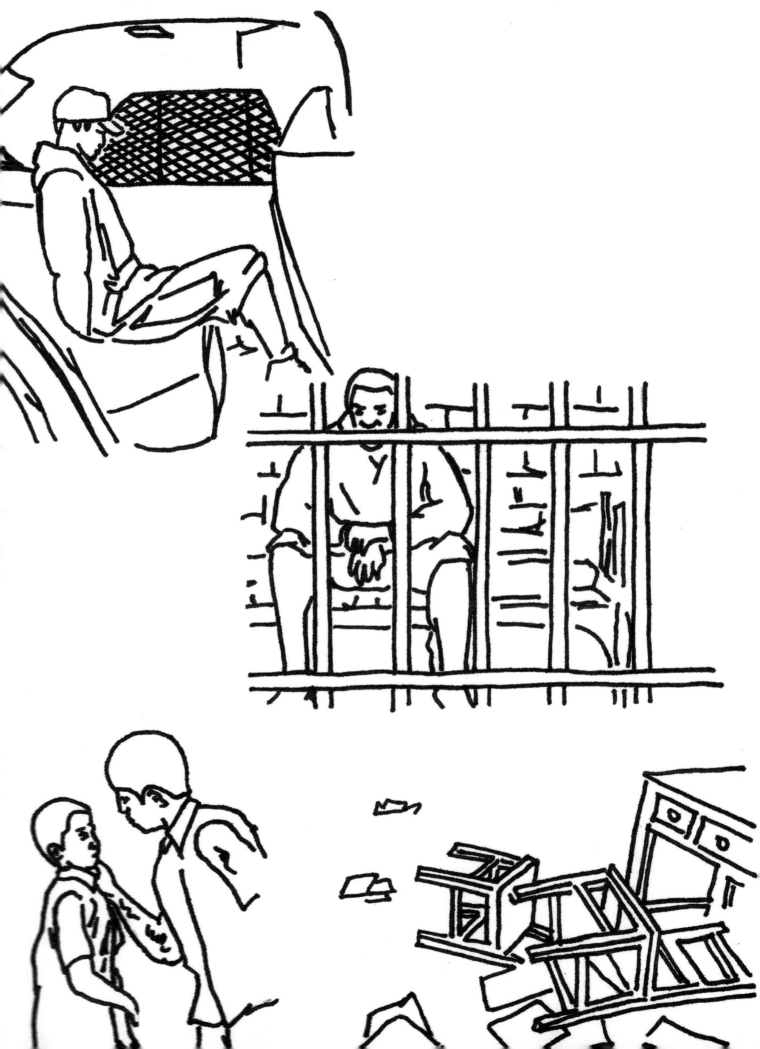

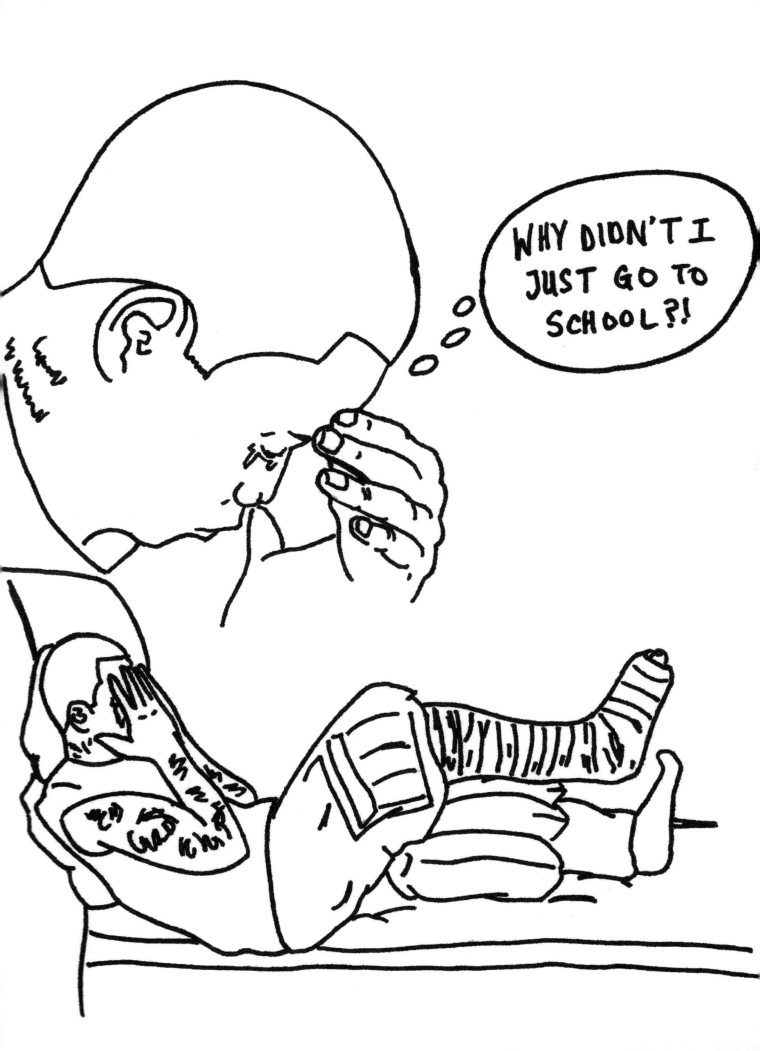

Printed in the United States
By Bookmasters